THE HUMMINGBIRD

MATT LONGABUCCO

The Hummingbird

POEMS

NIGHTBOAT BOOKS
NEW YORK

Printed in the United States

ISBN: 978-1-643-62328-3

Design and composition by Kit Schluter
Typeset in EB Garamond

Cataloging-in-publication data is available
from the Library of Congress

Nightboat Books
New York
www.nightboat.org

CONTENTS

NOCTURNES / NIGHT MEDS

1.

What's modern?
To live among roaches, among rats,
impulse control at the garden party,
a clock at such an enormous scale
entire generations never see it tick

Sober, steady talk while exiles
tear each other to shreds in a deserted club

This pizzeria got big online,
now they've hired someone to yell at my queen
about where on the sidewalk to stand
She doesn't make eye contact, takes one frosty step
Once, so high we had to hold onto the table edge,
she described plate by plate what was happening
to the food we couldn't finish: devastated eggs
in a congealed brown onion sauce, french fries
turning glutinous, top layer of the scooped-
out moussaka hardening to a crust

Then wondered in the cathedral if they really came
cloaked after hours to wail and spit on and lick the statues
in that town where under the great siege
remained not a single object to hurl over the walls

In the courtyard, bent for a dirty feather
determined to feel my biome,
my seethingness

Better to trade raving and the road for sorting, sharing?
Put an old t-shirt in the bin and watch
slim jim skins and wrinkly tomatoes collect on top
On a warm day the wire can in the park
wears a skirt of whatever teetered and tumbled down
If you would fain get swept up, you must first become trash

II.

Some have a gift for the passage of days in their average,
others an immunity
New humans pushing from the future
cast a long shadow over technique
One translation calls two years of wandering "desperate"
but the other says it's the wanderer himself who's "sick at heart"

Set up camp where nerves terminate
Trial I may have invented, for the reality nothing can be done
Don't forget the end of *The Age of Innocence*,
when you gossip about scandal you help weave the net
that will be used to constrain you, too,
should you ever decide to want something less vague
than what's wanted for you

Lately we're stiffs, avatars,
while in the next room our players argue logistics
and we wish what every avatar
has vainly wished: to dissolve back into the source
that was mud, that once braved the kiln

III.

Those honking geese would fit right in on Bushwick Ave
The risk of not stealing through the city
but becoming one of its fixtures
Shut out from every dwelling, lashed by a storm of hype
All the NYC Parks site reports about Willoughby
is that he married a Duffield, Brooklyn royalty

Where is security looser, usage down,
sunshine more on riverbank cascading?

So alone it's menacing or like some minor, deviant myth
Crossing fantasy, that lurching sea, tied fast with a rope
they held a lighter underneath, to fuse the knot
That clever man makes it home, he's so very weary,
but then...the suitors

If future loves exist, we're not permitted to know,
though knowing, we might take courage
Possibility resides in strangers
whose silence becomes a token or favor
You're far off, twisted in parties and perfume

Look, they're not sad poems, they're celebratory
they celebrate sadness
if celebrate means "find intricate"

Bike helmet claps my thigh the while
Hung it by a hook under the bar and later found
a soft gray mouse curled up inside, fast asleep
One obsession that serves as an ark for all the rest

IV.

Blandness has its day, purports to cover everything
She introduces her new beau on the street
and I forget not to snort when her friends say
they've heard so much about him

When I speak my love tells me to speak up
In the bookstore mutter the names
of world-historical poets not represented
on the shelf, like Petrarch who imagines that a person
seeing him in the aftermath of that affair
would recognize he'd been "just a little way from death"

I'm almost ready, let me do the dishes
and comb out the fern
Savored what I had when I had it but in the end
it didn't matter, eventually you have no choice
but to swallow the bolus, the mush
Even crushing has its customs
Can we check out the bar
where I think someone smiled at me once,
near where I buried a sickness whose half-life cooks the soil
Tar pits, undersea geysers, the whole bubbling bong of the earth
A thousand years from now
they call the whole city Smorgasburg,
no one remembers why

You've traveled ahead in time, the passage
retains your scent, I'd know it anywhere, lingering
like a grin at how we always arrive too late

v.

The clouds lower and everyone splits
A shell clings to me
or more precisely to a puckered membrane
I wear as a sheath,
the way one can hardly breathe inside one's fate,
beg the birds that chirp at dawn to clip it free

Poet who advises *make a list, make a list*
One person's disillusionment makes the other their stooge
By my count some of Odysseus's crew die three or four times
Unwelcome to anyone but an athlete
with a waist like a reed

Pain, the lover who calls at night
to wither resolve
A colleague's son died
People wander this food court
I get that I'm meant to think of them
as subjects of a technocratic order
but they're so baffled and hungry
The day this, the day that
The day did not cooperate
58 degrees, "feels like 44"
Fifty feels like the seafront churning by moonlight
This is a (fragmentary) poem to explain the interior
where mind is panicking that intimidation
knows our scent and is always the same
since that long-ago afternoon it first introduced itself
to a uselessly weak child's body,
then departed the scene before anyone else arrived
or just hid in the corner to stifle a sadistic fit

VI.

Flowers really do speak
I bought that bouquet of dried wild grasses
spiky puffs and petals
to loll in the vase day after day unchanging

In the Bywater, shot my mouth off about Bodhidharma,
how he declares, "If you're not sure, don't act"
Convinced myself and a few others
why this wisdom was to be followed
I hadn't brought the book with me
and only back home, reading further, arrived
at the page where he advises, "Act. Don't question"
and thought with alarm, I'd better make a few calls
to reactivate the inert and bid farewell to my own relief
over what in the name of least resistance
I'd failed to set in motion

The sudsy river
The lackadaisical wharf
I pick up an image, try to cash it in right away
Reading *There You Are* at A-Pou's Taste
thinking about mind's "back-and-forth, its lunar inconstancy,
its monkey leaps from branch to branch of the universe" per *Ka*
Bodhidharma says, "Understanding comes in midsentence"
Language finds its limit at the shop where "two sugars"
turns out to mean two sloppy ladlesful of syrup
"Honey cannot flow into the world without turning it upside down"
Pre-sunset
Stacked clouds
This time went for peonies that spend themselves
in a few short days of ragged, cunty glory

VII.

Strange, you read a poet again and again, all is opaque
then one day they die
and you open their book only to discover
the most bald confessions in the plainest language
or dire warnings, omens already come to pass

Loss-averse, trained in decisions but they're shrill, enacted
Come back to the evacuated scene of their initial assertion
to find the lost intervening time crumpled in a ball on the floor

This new paper crumples itself
and time appears like one of the gods
who falls out of an exhausted older god
in bright new armor
It doesn't mind being different, denser,
wants to requisition this space I've been using to exist
Feel it appraise the inner grooves, squeeze
the arteries, nest in the shaftways, rustle

So much pre-acting dumb
to secure one moment's convincing innocence
Every word is a sample,
an unfinished sentence, or lately
there's been a caesura in my speech,
my listener holds their breath upon the cusp,
worried I forgot my lines
Most paths descend to the tangles below,
except one poorly-marked trail that gives out
onto bluffs over open water

VIII.

We lurch to keep that story within the sayable
as the span of our attention has been measured and cut
My patience for optical illusions is thin
but I'd go see a few people hold forth until they drop

Characters are polite on television, acting the acting we do
Demure, I turn away to sip my drink
We get a table at the place where they use the animal so completely
the aperitif is its breath served in the delicate pouch of its lung

I'm planning this whole workshop to unearth a fairy tale
I don't know or only believed I knew
If the Fiend throws a photograph into the fire
it means all is condemned, not just the subjects
and what they're secretly thinking about each other
but also the pictured street or natural area,
any unlucky creatures or trees caught in the frame,
even the number used to tag the configuration
The Fiend can destroy a number, too, you're counting along
and then suddenly you reach it and *fafafafafa*

This is gonna be good, say the guards
When the whooping starts, it's music to their ears
Gnawing hunger, baying wolf, me and who
All the past is doing is making the ground unbreachable
New gesture is gazing toward the tops of the trees
but no higher

IX.

Luckily I'm not allowed to speak at the union bargaining meetings
I'm so prepared to cave at every moment
Anything to escape the conference room's terrible light

Plant me, then we'll see who comes to visit
Supposed to wait for the aftermath to write it down
Arrange things for later by this method
in the heads of friends and strangers
A shadow moves across the page
in the time it takes to coax a line
Romeo and Juliet's pact around misunderstandings
is meant to preserve their duet, its babble,
the way a few decisive touches set a world spinning—
Later on you're so helpless,
and no one needed to tell them this

On my shift, a kind-eyed woman burps the bags
of pizza dough, a shopper asks for Q-tips
while I'm stocking the Q-tips, I fumble the box,
she says she's sorry she disturbed my rhythm, giggles

Agamben says there comes a stage, late in life
when you at last bid farewell to your genius
that shadow or spirit whose nature is never to be fooled
and to dispense according to its inscrutable inclinations
wit, insight, the finesse of montage
It can't stay until the end, but shaped the host
through whom a characteristic sound can now be summoned
by any passing gust of air,
an amoral murmur like the underworld toil
meant to make tomorrow hospitable
Tomorrow, an island
Bath beside which some salt-stained rags
are left piled on the tiles
to be bundled away and burned

x.

What's modern?
Hashish journals, lepidoptery, gouaches, hydrotherapy clinics,
de profundis clamavi, one stocking pulled halfway up
the thigh and the other bunched below the kneecap,
descriptions of your character refracted through
characters that themselves require examination
in order to discern, not the you they describe
but the nature of their particular fascination, a feeling
sweet and fleeting as the drink that, soon emptied
and set down with a last rattle of ice, signals
goodbye and starting for home

From my bike whisper *don't kill me* to the trucks
Down avenue of the dead
where teeming thoughts are extruded
like organs from a corpse ready for mummification
using an instrument whose hook must be tapped
now and then against the lip of the jar
because the smegma of the liver half-pickled in life
has stuck stubbornly to the tong

No future
beyond a certain year floating in the near distance
Number we all know
or could make an educated guess at, give or take,
and so live backwards from there

In the end, this so-called marginal activity
turned out to be a threat
its enemies declare obsolete
Still, we trade away anonymity and awareness,
kneel to drink from the seep dampening the gritty wall
while somehow ignoring the divine torrent
that soaks every head
Let no mind catch fire
until every hungry mouth is fed

THE LOW TRUTH

HERE THE OLD rail line's nothing but
two faint joints in the road

clouds look stony, a mountain
seen from another mountain
if mountains reclined

want to believe so badly
barometric phases are what oppress us,
the groan of celestial wheels

this body's lived a life of its own,
was an instrument, could hardly
be commandeered, and only then
through shredded wires and collapsed tunnels
made to take one last look
at a definitive scene
in the moment before its demolition

a sick persistence kept me
in the land of the living

the hours didn't feel good
the days were okay
the minutes were bearable
the weeks were agony
the months were inane
the seconds were erotic and unsettling
the years terrific and mesmerizing,
stretching out children

then on Christmas Eve my barista,
my dentist, and the security guard from work
arrived each upon the chime of the clock
while a glaze was painted onto the streets

so much of a musical education was humiliation
now I listen in a locked room, in darkness

everyone's bold in their utterances
except a few who choose to murmur nonsense
onto obsolescent tape

wherever I sleep there's blood and it's mine

you aren't your beauty, or we set aside
the ways in which you are

confer exclusively about entanglements,
debrief regarding gestures
or seemingly inexplicable remarks

certain revelations are quicker to kill
than even the appearance of the miraculous

remember driving around with
four other guys all night, loud music,
blunts, the high squeal of masculine
tension, nothing to relish, grunting at
each other or sometimes venturing
into fraught subtlety, rituals prescribed
down to the placement and movement
of the fingers resting on one's own leg
or the timing of a laugh

and once, when summoned, I appeared
only to discover myself hours later, undone
in a zone of tan brick, the streetlights
blurred, sitting on the curb of a gas station
whose sign mimicked the color and font of BP
until I realized, those were not these letters

somehow sea and dust, lava and vortexes
make weather, childhood and longing
the unknown future, and the eyes
of the polis, disgrace

in *Woman on the Beach*
a stand of saplings, hidden in dunes
in a seaside town on the west coast of Korea
make Director Kim fall to his knees
struck by their youth, their distance from
one another, and the ontology of a trio,
not unlike the three steeples that set Marcel
to write the lines whose uncanny success
in capturing his sensation paradoxically
convinces him, in the throes of his first attempt,
that he'll never be a great writer

after all, one isn't a writer,
it's too long between the moments of writing

even the night is too long when we enter it

first noticed in *Hill of Freedom*
how Hong Sangsoo always leaves junk
and construction materials in the frame

the dogs in his movies are loved and lost,
abandoned and found

Director Kim is destructive in desire
but Mori from *Hill* is gentle and patient,
carries a book whose title is *Time*

he listens so carefully that he's able
to do the impossible, which is to stop talk
in its sometimes hypnotically insistent flow

and object to the principle of what's
being said or set the record straight
neutrally, almost helpfully

"you're a strange person"
a brusque man tells him

"you're strange, too" Mori replies,
as though it has just occurred to him,
right before the moment passes
in which a reply would still be possible

THETA

Θ

THEY'RE SAWING STONE up the block,
sluicing water over a circular blade,
when they take a break they leave the wide fabric hose
gurgling on the blacktop, laving the street,
pebbles embedded in asphalt catch the fading light
more readily seeming almost burnished or are they
in fact smoother, jutting out, exposed to our passing steps?

the same way I flip madly, searching for
a particular passage in a book I've stupidly insisted
we must consult before we can continue

obviously, I've been ill, turn around
and my death's not bigger, just closer—
that's no window, it is his leviathan eye,
the apparent storm its heaving fluid,
he blinks like someone pulling the shade
with a misplaced force that snaps it open again

you're downplaying what a good time
you're having on your trip?
please, I invented that move

Θ

it's the dead, they've read everything,
they're brandishing the books with rage

there should be an independent book fair
in Tartarus (another one)

have poets been lying, all this time, about correspondences?
lying and picking my pocket while they did

you've given it up, I notice, but publish away
in an alternate dimension (I confess, it's real to me)
where volumes fall from the sky, choke streams,
hit unsuspecting cattle on the head, or land in desert expanses,
wind riffling the pages

sometimes picture getting clipped by a car
in the street, how easily this body full of memories
would turn to dry snapping wood and leaky bags

showered with blossoms, I was once a vessel
for a joy so pure it bordered on the malign

by the bike pump refuse to admire the fitness
of twentysomethings—I was fit then, too,
and used to fall asleep on the train, waking far down
the line where it is neither underground nor elevated,
but trundles along in the dirt

we used to try to creep by time itself
when it thought we slept, and closed its eyes
for a second like one does for fun on the road,
while somehow the clasp of that necklace,
in the recess, rewound all the way from clavicle to nape

now when I try to get the dawn light on my face
it won't accumulate, in the bathroom
the translucent green moth waits where I let it survive,
trapped (my love language), probably making
the toothbrush cup its redoubt

Θ

today the A is an F
seatmate sings *runnin' with the devil* in a high baritone
ten-year-old on the platform
throws a handful of rose petals as hard as he can

the absolute delicacy of the simulation,
the deadpan expression,
"indescribable composure" (Turgenev),
this machine can show you anything
but shows you gaping at it too,
trying to see knowledge from above
like straining to see what's fluttering too close
to your eye, or impossibly up inside the edge of a frame,
memories hold something real but recede,
answers await in the swarm of them, also the risk
of sticking one's hand in the whirring machine
from which a tangle of tape designating
the since-that-moment-unsaid spools forth,
loops and sticks, penetrates its own jumble
causing further loops while at the same time
being delicate enough to bend or tear,
with a chitinous color that suits its ceaseless rattle

these people so fit and polished, who know and have
what's good in life, now stake out and claim depravity too,
so what's to seek? it will have to be sadness, sickness,
failure steaming in a pot, you hold your nose
and from the ladle, with all of us watching, take a sip
that makes a decade vanish somewhere

quit, spend, show off, but if your ambition isn't big enough
you might catch up to it, catch it, and they'll say
there you go, enjoy

Θ

mixed blessing, fraud investigator bought a copy of my book

Rovelli calls the quantum world *agitated and fluctuating*,
from the deepfake emerges the incontrovertible,
astringent as ginger billowing through the head

pleasure is weak and mistakes turn heavy,
you arrive at a gravity that lasts only for a time
(perhaps an accident mars it)

wanting, then stranded wanting,
faces are issued blank until stamped, set,
static in the tunnel, retraining for the now,
ensorcelled scrolling this core sample of whims,
full moon ebike ride, cardiac arrest edge play at the gym
but I'm not trying to expire on Fulton
across from SuperFoodtown

relieved by that loss, you punish yourself
for a feeling soon indistinguishable from genuine grief,
now if someone tells me about their midlife reckoning
I answer yes, yes, we're made of star stuff and burnt letters,
there are gems that drink light and cry glamour
and there's the emptiness they say artisans incorporated
deliberately into the pattern of the finest lace

Θ

New Year's Eve
my daughter texts from her room across the city
(the lonely Longabuccos),
at my place we start but don't finish
Fabian: Going to the Dogs
Rachel declares neither of us will ever really
be a writer, then passes out

as for that thing I'm going to write,
it's difficult to categorize, benefits from
the habit of being picked up and opened
to a random page, is a building
or body buckling from the center
and at the same time quick, jangly,
an attack of throwing stars in the courtyard
amid cherry blossoms expiring
upon the path already littered
with messages disguised as banalities
but inscribed in the blue ink
that means *come tonight*

Θ

want to see something? watch these two interact,
they haven't spoken in years,
now she's going to cross the bar and he's not going to flinch

someone asks me to trust them but as with a fox
peeping out at a nice-seeming hand for sniffing,
all evolution tells me to back away
like I reel from people in line at the bank behind
velvet ropes that form a geometric path
orchestrating a dance subtle and elaborate
as one performed in a minor court in the provinces
whose every rite is fueled by a desire
to make your rivals faint at the sight of your name

the mysteries consist of "the saying of
many ridiculous things and many serious things"
don't I myself live in the capital?
smeared with impressions

meaning flows down from a source within the palace,
almost from the forehead of the sovereign,
but democracy, any household's reckoning, compiles
its own signs, melancholy, deliberate as only the clumsy
resolve to be, pulling on defiance like a workshirt
and ending every night stone drunk

Θ

pspspspsps

first unhappy morning in a perfect world

no one's ever mouthed anything to me
that the whole room didn't see

aging, resisting trajectories of sameness while the city
threatens to replace everything I find interesting
with everything I don't

Pan abides in nature's sounds, our startled reaction to them

passion's onomatopoeia, sad clown in hideaway socks

"For a moment confusion reigned over time"
is how I'd translate that line of Enrique Lihn

people tightening their delusions, twisting two sharp wires into one

what's your name, anyway?
                                        Phaedra
                                                        oh damn

ϴ

why can't you read my book on the train?
because of the poor reception

sorry for those sonnets,
I tried to write a poem by speeding up reading
as I neared the end of yours, thinking I'd be able to
somehow leap into my own from there

but you'd sealed the final line the way
you hid definitiveness in your casual goodbyes,
I never texted you first or you'd accuse me
of doing it out of the blue

Θ

I saw him concentrating—
pinball's so strange, waiting out the reveries

mosquitoes prefer your blood,
drive you indoors, I stay and watch wax fold over
itself with our friend who studies the calligraphic arts
in these studios, wears painter's pants flecked
strictly with ink, we bring in a pizza, paper plates
come apart from one another with a crack

when everyone's asleep I turn on a single lamp,
read four pages each from seven books,
next morning river's so gray you almost warn the villagers
stooped washing their clothes on the banks

after the bond gives way, truth oozes out, you finally glimpse
in the mirror what you used to search for in its surface
when you spaced for an hour at the sink

Θ

morning, bowl of seeds steeped in the milk of the oat

resent even those blades of grass that grow between us,
rain over prairies or wrapped around mountains
thwarts reception, makes you flicker or freeze in my dreams

a girl circles her beach blanket eating
a very flat hamburger, a rosary of Sicilian seaweed
spent the winter in the pocket of my trunks

funny business, holding on to a feeling,
reminding yourself, but somehow not needing
a reminder for the reminder, to feel it

nose starts bleeding and my weirdness is all over my hands

don't open my suitcase
or notebooks
hauled my whole laboratory to withering—sorry—
withering—fuck—wuthering heights

earth sign crushing on a gale
"sleepwalk" on repeat

I'd be okay being near people, if these really are people,
despite the enthusiastic rhythms of their speech

some exercise their mad devotion in mental cabinets
no one can ever check

stay a few extra days, next week is slow
and you're soaked
we see the woman cutting flowers and know Mr. Keats has died

don't just remember me, that only works for nine years

Θ

where am I? in a hushed hell of expectation
with a devil who loves to hum

the alternative is to drown in silence,
swimming upstream there's never a breath
that's all air, as the past gags us with the solution
in which it was preserved in case the chance
to complete its inkling of splendor ever arrived

the devil's only read one book but it's *Proust and Signs*
by Gilles Deleuze (tr. Richard Howard), it says
ideas enter us by way of sorrows, and describes
"the intelligence that undergoes the pressure
of signs and comes to life only to interpret them,
in order thus to exorcise the void in which it chokes,
the suffering that submerges it"

my therapist asked whether my dream of journeying
deep underground might signify, not a death wish,
but rather a search for precious ore
"Am I supposed to answer that question?"
"You're not *supposed* to do anything"

Θ

do they think I've been in the toilet too long?
did it catch on to watch live feed
of people in their apartments
from cameras in the corner of every room?

stitching, inking, warped by loneliness,
flying at others before I even knew
what others were

hard to say what these setbacks do to you, exactly—
don't say make you stronger—
it's rather that things feel possible
only because you got left behind in some easier place,
doing long jumps on the moon
(novels never seem to require explication anymore),
and the thing you didn't get, or person let down
or stumbled before are back on earth
where wind rushes over the Azores bringing more
new time, flexible and strong, to be marked by everything
then lay coiled for the remainder of eternity
bound to hold the impression

Θ

late, even the moon closes out

leave my glass on a tabletop
so clean and dark it's like placing it in space,
tilt my head so she won't light my nose
along with my cigarette

opaque with exploits,
but it will still be hours before we can cast a shadow

did those things actually happen?
no one ever mentions them and they changed
the name of the neighborhood where most of them
would have occurred

saw a bee *walking* up Sixth Ave
spray at the crest of the fountain does something like repeat

one day not a flicker of approval,
the next one of those heart icons so big and red
you blush when it appears

then this book says they're not even my desires
try to take them from me and we'll see

Θ

someone's laugh rings out in ripples

in paradise we clump up, swim

from the bark on my back I pass you a chip

the temple, the garden,
a person putting in eye drops supplies a statue

stay for the glimpsing, like immortals equipped
to do nothing else but part branches, trade looks

too much abrupt leaving of rooms,
was it lame to act bored at Café Triste?

you dreamt you were kept to be skinned and eaten

in my dream was a rivulet of fast-flowing dirt
into which I plunged my hand and felt the grainy surge

Θ

woman announces she got her hair cut
and everyone in the cafe looks up

kid on bike to his dad, "how are you
supposed to stop *not* out of nowhere?"

cuirass of bark falls free with a clatter,
sun won't set, hydrangeas hold their glow

my favorite person in Brooklyn is still the clerk
who boxed up that piece of cake with such deliberation—
by all means, trim the string

crew at East Coast Mechanical are nice to old ladies,
in my anecdotal report

choose between two possibilities by the same method
I used when I was six, from crosswalks gawk
(if I'm looking away from you, we're in love already)

would be happiest riding shotgun on a road trip,
careless and high, but these days who could bear me,
who could I bear, and how could I be empty enough
for sparks of destiny shearing away
to leave theta, the death's head, scorched across my chest

change of seasons only reminds me of our year, its fugue,
pretend for form's sake to have subjects,
don't bother dispelling fictions in which I'm depicted
sleepy with comforts or mired in care

goodnight from New York City
which is in some sense a bone, a shell

goodnight, wherever you are,
being so smart it hurts

Θ

droplet tumbled a long way
from clouds surmounting clouds
to land in your gleaming hair

spasm that comes upon me, halfway
through drawing a straight line by hand

listen now, the last of the summer notes

late likes

do-nothing days
and hand-cranked curiosity

"my heart the bazaar"—Pessoa

Bill Hader says, about receiving feedback,
that people are always right when they tell you
something's off, and always wrong
in their idea about how to fix it

DOGWOOD

UNKNOWING AT THE outset
Unknowing at the source
Do the most important thing
Keep a diary
Half you, half everything else

This leaf turns red with all it saw
Or actually buds, it's spring
Occurrences are pigments
The spirit a clacking wheel
Apocalypse is tasteless and tiresome
Ideas deteriorate, decay
Except when upon some propitious cusp
A new subject emerges
Salt-flecked and dripping from the sea
Fourth-grade teacher couldn't hide his disdain
For the Trojans, so by implication taught us
To align with Fate
Embarrass ourselves in passion
Play it cool at the shops

Rachel asks if I'm her friend or her nemesis today
Smokes and inspects the fake food we bought
Images dissolve in the bloodstream
Snow falls on the lake
Or no, springtime, vases unpacked and dusted
Two friends or roommates brought their taxes
To the cafe where one shows the other
Something on her phone
The friend without turning or looking
Says *that's so cute*, I scratch out a line
Breeze ruffled your hair the wrong way
Is how I knew it was a dream
Watching you delete, with bruising commentary
The set of pictures I took
Thinking later I'll recover

Season of backlit blossom flurries
Some work alone
Some cry relation, relation
Girlfriend sees boyfriend drag their dog by its leash
Hey, you said we shouldn't do that
Consider the volcano couple
Their commitment to costumes and rigorous study
Even or especially in the zone of death
By fire, think of it
I always just assume we'll drown

It's not that I'm shy and shitty
It's how often people guess wrong
About which I'm being with them
Ikkyū writes *nobody knows shit*
nobody lives anywhere hello dust!
The terms we use, the energy we need
Can only be concocted fresh
From each day's new-stocked store of possibilities
That by nightfall's a ransacked or abandoned room

Entertain an idea to compile a list
Of all rhetorical questions asked by poets for the past twenty years
And answer them all, No
Like digging for treasure, the shovel
Shushing through dirt suddenly rings on metal
And everyone locks eyes
Or a couple reads next to each other, one laughs
Long expectant pause
Waiting in vain for habit to dull my worship
Doesn't the body shudder when the soul breaks into flower?
No

Malka wakes up from the ketamine they use for anesthesia
To what she calls an epiphany
About the greatness of woman doctors
Spontaneously hugs the oral surgeon

Who is momentarily taken aback before reciprocating
Day so bright I fold away my reading glasses
Cop tickets a silver 'vette
Air hardens in the tube of the pump
Until one's full weight can hardly force it into the tire
Tree that never shed its thick brown lobed leaves
Wraps them cloak-like around itself
In the teeth of the wind off the river

Crowd leaves the station, I missed a train
Where thick rubber panels of subway car floor are torn
They've administered a line of rivets whose broad heads
Hold fast both edges of the wound
If I see someone I know, I'm boned
Cartridges everywhere
Skyscrapers/syringes is that anything?
Smoking on the hill in the breeze by the river
In other words bringing together all 4 elements
Trying to achieve a fifth

Entertain the idea to compile a list
Of things I could talk about all day
The works of Andrea Arnold or the notion
In *Time Tells* that certain films of our youth
Whether good or bad contain a quality of presence
No longer available except through its refraction
In these artifacts almost seeping with its still-potent joy

At the very last school they taught me logic
Is a dangerous lie you should deride wherever it appears
And refuse to look away from what fear of pain distorts
Affront the hateful with compassion
At the same time relentlessly mock and challenge them
Call violence by its name
Though it means you'll never rest
Costume idea, the protagonist from *La Jetée*, army jacket
And styrofoam eye patches, plus hammock to bite

His gift is how vividly he feels the past
It gets him killed

Dog comes by, as usual I stiffen
We're both relieved when his owner trails back
To ask if he's making friends
They could land a plane by the glare of notebooks
Laid open along this riverbank
The city's name must travel far, attract scribes
Humid, public, indiscreet
Spring, right, they repaint the benches, bleachers
You stroll over to find me reading your post
We do an unwitting vaudeville routine
Till it becomes clear you've never actually
Heard of the Circle Line

Dad to late arrival, *we'd almost given up on you*
Dad who when his kid's wad of gum tumbles to the sidewalk
Doesn't miss a beat before saying *easy come, easy go*
Burl of that woman's laugh
Ringing out as her girlfriend's mumble
Occasionally hastens to produce it in her
On the arch above the entrance to the Rose Reading Room
"A good Booke is the pretious lifeblood of a mafter fpirit
imbalm'd and treafur'd up on purpofe to a life beyond life"
Slumped fiddling with my phone
In a wooden phone booth with a foldable door
Old encyclopedia fucks with subtraction
Heals when you don't use it for a while
Within a month you have to cut the pages all over again
Life beyond life?

Desperate entreaties stretched taut over bones
Thereby made visible, as in those Schiele drawings
Where nude flesh is barely a sheet thrown over death
Drawings are organisms to which an involved looking gives birth
Remain alive until the final stroke is made

At which point they desiccate, leaving their prized residue
Squalor will unquestionably prevail
We'll have to shake off all the harder its gloomy feeling
And presentiments of general disposal

A boy says *that's a horse*, gazing at a bronze statuette
Of a horse, Greek, 2nd century BC
The mom's boyfriend replies *that's not a horse, it's a lamprey*
And laughs in a way that makes
Me retroactively take note of the exchange
There are backward joints
Perspectives whose wrongness jolts the eye
The veracity of this Cycladic harp player, 2800 BC,
    has been questioned
Because depictions of musicians are rare in the period
But I'd prefer its veracity be confirmed, please

Why must everything pass through my age
Come up behind Tenaya in Shake Shack
(It's all one fictional day)
Whisper, *I know what you're doing*
That is, using the special discount code he told us about
Some night, and which I now use too, sparingly
Every few weeks so as not to draw suspicion
He laughs and says, *I wondered if anyone wrote it down*
Yeah, me, and several times a practically free meal
Has been a relief, *anyway my daughter's over there*
I'm gonna go back and sit, but let me know
If you want to talk about setting up a reading at Purgatory

Stonehouse says he lives in a maze of peaks
Hillman claims the dead whisper
Because their lack of materiality
Causes a loss of certainty in their speech
Larded, as a result, with *as* and *like* and *seem*
Missing my friend, lately
That's where the other half of the G train is, in a way

People drag forth their families to be glared at by ghouls
We leap over one astonishing moment
Then turn back to stare dumbfounded at the fossil it's become
Even the houseplant, to marry the watering can
Wants to abandon its roots
But their intricacy is time itself
Doesn't the possibility of a turn originate
Within the very marrow of the hinge?
No

Register one of those perceptible shifts in our dynamic
After complaining our days are too short
Or too sped up by wine
Those times someone challenged my story about myself
I went crazy
Couldn't shut the lights but felt they must be covered
Now they blaze forth from around irregular patches
Precisely understood distances between people
Precisely who's lording it over whom
The golden rule, but I don't want anything done to me
Unto me
The lesson was meant to emphasize a metrical passage
But these scholars always overstate the stresses
No matter how tranquil the speech
Wind never sleeps
Can we just for a second
Wait wait WAIT
Stir oatmeal, pour tea
Constant work is one of the inescapable realities
Shakes its leg, thumps the table

Getting passed over
Well, don't stand at attention now
Whoever adores the master too much
Becomes disciple, then assistant, is finally dismissed
The instant the real hero arrives
In the forbidden annex I hear the garble
Of a guard's walkie-talkie coming closer

Tracking, it turns out, a bolder thief
Stealthy, gracile, she darts right past me
My coat's the color of limestone
And I was taught by a sage practitioner to keep still
No matter how my impulses dance

Things I could talk about all day
Kisses on film, kisses in bars
Those sweet kisses laid along the torso
By a lover sinking down
Soft parts squashed against the ribs, against the spine
Eyes meet, but in the mirror, so it doesn't count
Loneliness, who can take it, not me
Do these louts realize I arrived at this party
Having correctly predicted several outfits?
Down to the item and provenance?

Transformed into an animal by your foot upon the stair
Lines shrugged off and strewn across the floor
You had me at matte finish
Wash my eyes, redden their rims
Collect the razors that putt-putt down the avenue
The wind wants to be in poems
Spring o spring
Witness some dogwood drama at the park
Rain-washed cars and streets
Deep puddles from the flood

Hand pulling free of the hand that grasps it
Isn't even weakness
It's, it's cosmic
The universe isn't only expanding out there
You're that, too
Meet me in the one place that matters
The chamber
Or, the open?
No, the chamber

NO TITLE MEANS IT'S SPIRITUAL

says Eileen

obviously, we take no vows

clip onto the great chain of being to ride downtown

set loose by spasmodic demand
we're hopeless liars
forborne by right of exhaustingly elaborate excuses
no one has the wherewithal to check

it isn't that, being frozen,
we should over a lifetime melt,
become a puddly fen watched until,
upon the late-morning evaporation
of the final molecules of dew,
grasses flush a green so deep
parallel universes become visible
passing in front, motley and chaotic,
but that like all ice in this sweltering,
coughing age of combustion, we lack
the ability to solidify, cohere

was it a spontaneous feeling
or a trope or veneer of improvisation
laid over a familiar frame

wish you were bored, available

love these changing social mores (morays?)

Akerman: *I am a teenager no more,*
how is that possible?

walking down Myeongdong with my earbuds

once she sort of teetered on her heels—
now whenever I see someone teeter on their heels
I want to talk with them, ask them what it's like

laconic diary of the empirical
my community service is investigative and oral

one day's ration of desperate wishing

all I can tell her, arm her with, is someone cares
so fucking much what happens to you

on hillock where ten picnic blankets
join to lay claim

trying to arrange concealment
over concentration, almost without detection
leads toward the aesthetic of horror or an adjacent
durational genre we might simply call fear instead

the devil, medium-dicked and mean,
screws the camcorder onto the tripod

revelation at the wine-god's festival,
suddenly each spoke with the voice of another

person behind me in the revolving door pushes,
handle floats away from my hand

but forgetting is an action

so much labor's needed to truly fail

trapped in life-writing
do not pay me

stores don't give out bags anymore
so we see everyone's groceries,
their wine and beans

"I feel hemmed in by these provincial places"
"South Brooklyn?"

what a single day counting for something
would mean, in the hospice where
the living retreat to the parking lot
to take cigarettes in gulps

but everyone's kind,
gives advice, recs, praises stumbling
in the highest terms

Carson: *People need acts*
of attention from one another,
does it really matter which acts?

let's spoon
marking each micro-chronic shift
with a note, thereby accidentally
composing all human songs

like William IX
I'll send you the poem,
you send me back its key

not looking to be the laureate of aches and pains

tried to sort of hook my context onto my thoughts
but could see, giving the result a gentle push forward,
how the parts were falling off, rolling away

past the waterfront development
these bland knowledge-workers
funded and pretend to share

past half-torn branches
like messages that arrive shredded

past the fool's fort of breezes,
the smoke in cars still in the parking lot
of the hospice

where a last chance remains
to fathom the visitor,
even while the carts
go rattling through the ward

STUDENT OF INSTITUTIONS

THE BOTTLE SAID bliss
but inside was *cold quicksilver sweat*
it soaked the floor
though no one was in sight, unless empty elevator cars
across the lobby were wormholes,
like a supernova collapsing or one of the places
on Flatbush you can make a left

because you raised your hand to float free
you must be stitched to yourself, pinioned,
dyed the color of rocks, dust in pant cuffs,
the final platelet bearing an extinct affection

I want to heal completely, one last time,
and then—
oh, then you're done?
oh I'm John fucking Donne

- - - - -

should I smoke this, knowing
for every moment I've acted the robot
I'll pay dearly, all at once?

long convo with a closed door,
the high probability of becoming
ridiculous in some way

"No great life is complete without
a trial, you have to ruffle a few feathers,
you can't just be a good little child
all your life," insists this autofictioneer,
claims she could seduce anyone
after she realized everyone is bored
and waiting for something to happen

what about those periods of going
through the motions, even proudly?
can it be the noticeable itself retreats,
folds in? love doesn't barely miss us:
no asteroid almost punches through
the shield of the sea

everything natural remains neutral,
we make it complain,
they say nothing but bloodshed
can compel the shades to step from the fog
and beg too late
to lay again beside a body in such a way
that every corresponding part touches
(only available on earth)

- - - - -

wanted this juice until faced with it

"winter negroni" (they add emergen-C)

I'm for you and adore you,
watch you at your watch, voyeur of
a scowling voyeur, servant and pimpernel
making adjustments, hand-arranging
the pebbly shore because you prefer
wet rocks, abhor the sight of them
dry and dulled with salt

dark day or light night, keep
polar hours, every reading I assign
sooner or later reveals its violence,
trace of our great psychopathy,
freeze frame of anyone laughing

or gulping—I broke the back
of my skull against a beam

decorated in the name of reclamation
with rivets and tar

- - - - -

that torn-apart poet reads everywhere,
slips and staggers, is almost ashamed
of having granted the world any sanity
to begin with and okay, accept the villains
are interchangeable, what's harder is
to scratch out roles and structures,
but can we try, with blades?

more likely we'll wind up drinking
out of the gutter, knowing our drink
was pure rain until it passed over
these surfaces, more human efforts

the way the tempest roared
in the nightmare about a tidal wave
that, from the cliff where I watched,
swallowed the whole terrified shore of
the beloved—not that different from
the genocide and being awake

- - - - -

unprompted crit: he likes to Build a Creature

shiny face, sartorial flair, eight-pointed glint
spiraling in and out of your eye,
bottomless pack of cigarettes within reach,
your unruly hair reminds me of the film
I couldn't coax back onto the spool,
or the celluloid spilling out of its groove
reminds me of your wild hair

calm my hormones, as they used to advise

we admire the serious and capable,
who require no guile

I'll write lines for us both, but first steal
the curtain so it's like the play can't legally end

- - - - -

the book's implicit question:
could you live with nothing, even now?

twenty-pound genetically modified rat
in striped pants, on Gates, insists offering up
one's desire as if it were somehow constitutive
of the self is the coward's way out

an old friend whose longtime partner died
saw me, on the one-year anniversary,
told me her life was over, let me know
I'd let her down

I'd be better as a thing,
or a pile of money everyone could take
a handful of, to convert into comfort

an absorbent capsule
meant to bear away some poison, in the end,
from the total that taints the earth

I'm guarded,
that's what I should have said in my defense,
but things can't be guarded,
you can hate and break them, if you own them,
you can punish them
or do whatever you please

- - - - -

it's me, post-reunion, who gives up
and stops calling, can't figure out
how to keep it going

hand in hand at the reading
where the ground split and swallowed
us whole, then spit out these replicas
and cursed them with stamina, that delusion

winding our way back
from the outskirts to the volume
to top up everyone's memory of us
as the ones unwilling to head home

stingy architecture, spigots of wine,
we had so long and asking was always mellow,
couched in a joke
or mollified by a knowing look
(but that's just eyes meeting)

we're going to require a declaration
"Since he has something to lose, he is
condemned to prudence," says
a famous shrink, and another, "What is
an obsessional? All in all, he is an actor
playing his part, carrying out a number of
acts as though he were dead. It's a way
of shielding himself from death"

shaky coast
madness after the thaw
overwhelmed by a fugitive trace

- - - - -

so nervous about what I'm saving for last

big whooshing copy job in silent library,
the joke became, every time Bahaar asked me
if I'd read a book, I would say I'd "looked at it"

me and a guy touch fingers, both reaching
for the Stop Requested button—
with a stoner's exaggerated tact I step away,
crumpling my beanie in my hands

Rachel must be home, always leaves
her shoes in the hallway right left
instead of left right

said I'd been working like a dog lately
and she laughed, but in fact
I've been writing what might be
a third of something, trilogies love me
though all they can do is arc, disappoint

at this point the crime show
is survivors stumbling around, episode
after episode, getting blackout drunk

city worker tries to start a chainsaw
but for now only clears its throat

- - - - -

the night is rubber, it's lycra,
our shadows in zoetropic motion
on the wall, pleasure by agenda item but
when it came time to introduce new business
I shook my head, unsure

I'm ashamed of my late discoveries,
prefer your way of leading, letting me space

and stay muted, burning broadsides
when the temperature drops

cold island between us
or it's a bare room where
for some reason we're obliged to meet
while outside our feelings crowd
and delight in each other like friends
encountered in unexpected places

walk out of here with me,
I know you think you won't find your way back
but I promise, what you are isn't this
or any location but a series,
careening, not glued to the spot watching
time pass overhead with its horrible lining
of what didn't happen and was left undone

inside its sock or sleeve
is the sky, flower-blue, our favorite molecules
in their long fragrant chains

- - - - -

on the sidewalk, smashed ballpoint,
intact spring rolls free

this bookstore makes no fucking sense,
what do you mean these are the originals?
what do you mean they all are?

now I'm at "writing night"—
listen, I've tried everything—
smoking outside, staring at a discarded
yogurt cup bobbing upside-down on the surface
of a bowl full of rainwater set for no
imaginable reason beside the curb

such barometers spontaneously appear,
it's still beautiful to pollute,
ebikes minnow behind the undercover car
revealed now by its flashers

people notice my principled restraint
and slowly refine their own online activity as a result

new poets simply arrived last, it's all that matters

I guess snow on mountaintops melts
and becomes fast-running unfordable-for-a-time
cold refreshing streams below?

- - - - -

those clips are really playing the flagpole

the breeze exists to equalize
what's over here
with what's over there—
the procedure is the relief

a drone disappears behind the tree, and we to it

skeptical of a five-year-old's loudly proclaimed
four-leaf-clover discovery I crane my neck,
the dad who sees my eyebrows rise scowls back

the piece of hate inside everything
is there to turn our heads toward humility
and with it our obscure and arduous journey,
letting go the way the space around it
lets go of a tree in imperceptible negative rings
that technically diminish its vast remnant
while cauterizing with irreversibility's heat
the edge it believes itself to need

it takes a thousand lifetimes per person
to set things right—no, not just with your friends

- - - - -

that everyone's connected
is what gets you in the gorge

lots of those knots that tighten if you move

I'd been performing a spell
to protect myself from bad feelings
by turning them into whiskey
and taking them in that form
like painting the inside of my head

only to awaken in Parque México,
cool cement and purple blossoms,
nearest frisbee player to me
sported fingerless gloves and wouldn't run
even a few steps to catch misthrows,
preferred to let the disc clop and scrape
along the ground

- - - - -

in my coffin, reposting mentions

cruising this bickering couple
at times the key to seducing anyone
hangs forgotten from its hook by the door

Satan slides the satisfied off his enormous belly
onto hot spikes

lays a leathery palm on each soldier's brow,
finds an unswept temple and repairs through

a crack in the floor no wider than a hair
that winds up in your mouth and must be
scraped with difficulty from the tongue

intimacy: you send me a piece
still 300 words over the count,
tell me *do what it takes*

RIP Gustave Flaubert
you would have loved track changes

out behind the venue,
between sets of the dragon dance,
the back legs bum a smoke
from the woman who whips the tail,
yesses arrive in the wind off the harbor,
water totally unaware it's ever rippled before
ripples just fine, betrayal is prefigured
by betrayal, I scare a bike, scare myself,
skeptical of free will but karma is all around,
we know it as color and flavor and
the unnerving motion of these insects
that concentrate its ultimata
into the panic of a single day

THE HUMMINGBIRD

>>

DRAW CURVES AND scooped forms
from the volume outside the window
where a bee drops into cup
after cup   an all-day drunk

S lets us house-sit upstate
while she birdwatches in South Jersey
from the faithful RV
we once stood inside to admire
“wow, it’s bigger than you think”

I’m not prepared for the excellent quality
of her high-powered binoculars   and these are just
the home pair   so sensitive they need bracing
or the jumping image makes me seasick

through them a hummingbird
    unlike the one who refused
to alight, earlier   perches a moment
on the feeder’s lip

what’s magnified is more real
    Pessoa says freedom
is freedom to contemplate by sight alone

I won’t become a bird watcher
but perceive its absorbing influence
    the markings, habits, heraldry
a glittering demimonde
glimpsed behind tall, forbidding hedges
or from the boulevard through a closing gate

>>

one loves effect, tolerates cause
drags a dipstick across the pond
onto whose surface paint of many colors was poured
until an elegant paisley appears

everything's drifting around, nervy
and entangled   seed pods, cigarette smoke
ashes I watch sift down from the secluded
second-story deck   liquid Hudson Valley evenings
when a red lighter's luminous against wall-to-wall green
continual croaking and shrieking in the trees

it rained earlier, then it rains
on every channel at once, but we're already inside
luscious pages when tilted toward
the light reveal faint, damp indentations
where my fingertips rested a moment too long
against the fibers

I'm peeing   "beaded bubbles winking at
the brim"   when you appear in the bathroom's
opposite door, having come through
the office where you raided the CD towers

like the Lintons we cast a shadow on the picture window
are a Heathcliff and Cathy huddled out there
watching us dance to Prince and blast The Who?

>>

concerning the lifespan of rewards
or reward-enjoying there is an etiquette
“Have we ever done this?”
“I think I’d remember if we had”
“And this?” “Definitely not”

the clay pots are wet, or wet again   thyme and basil leaves
their deepest green   rose of sharon magnificent
    tomato plants clench their roots against the deluge
they’ll slurp up later to brew their juice

summers are sad now   and the temperate, we understand
was always a miracle, our name for what
nature only does once

recall trips when after the nuisance of an appointment in town
you discover the others have already had their day in the sun
    decide to go anyway while they nap and read
visit alone the late afternoon beach
the sea suggests a menacing intelligence at work
determined to sift every grain

back at the house, still out of sync
    come in sandy and surly to find them
embarked on drinks and dinner prep
    you head up to shower
but first sit at the edge of the bed in the dark
doting on an impossibility
you keep scrupulously to yourself

>>

windows are unreal
    frames for a waking dream

is what guides the hummingbird
closer to a pang or a thrill?   this one's
yellow stripe's dull and spotty as the double line
down a worn winter road

a fly butts the glass pane, I mistake
the sound for R rapping at the door with
a knuckle but when I look up she isn't there
    return to my work, as I call it without conviction

the hummingbird and I are always hungry
    each creature has its degree of skittishness
knows how quick or ever-moving or patient
it needs to be, in direct relation to the style
of its predators, their own relative speed
and flair for acceleration   or capacity
to blend in and stalk

a fly butts the glass pane, I mistake the sound
for R rapping at the door with a knuckle
but when I look up she isn't there
    return to my work, sewing costumes
for one of those rushed, timid skits
where a few stand in for all
as if each thing didn't stand for another

try to define analogy
you'll soon be in deep water
    try to guess the lottery numbers
you won't succeed   better to invent a system
that operates on the difference between your numbers
and the future winning combination
until that difference has been reduced to zero

>>

mid-afternoon, possibility, vagrancy
    shifting of furniture, divvying
up of light and shade, blood sugar's
pitch and roll, what the proud or melancholy
call interiority   breaking down food into nutrients
until what has been dispossessed
of the nutrients it bore is precisely shit

hard not to believe some judicious force
turns my talent up and down with a knob
depending on how much I am myself

finicky rain, humidity, the sun goes down
    AC set to outer space
the present exhausts, evaporates
    from time to time one must leave it
to make more marks

>>

from the conservatory I text about dinner ideas
    split tree across the yard attests
lightning's work is bold, permanent

R's in true posthuman form   thumb a blur
above her phone   smokes, laughs at someone's
message in a way that makes my stomach hurt

to make the hummingbird disappear
simply lift the binoculars from the table
    the background panoply gives no help

Slim the cat slips through the wet grass
    "When a vast part of what existed
withdrew into the invisible, this didn't
mean it stopped happening. But it became
easier to think it wasn't happening"

we know about tulip mania
but this article says a scholar
must dutifully report, historically (what else?)
it never actually occurred   removing at a stroke
certain load-bearing premises
    find the needle in the haystack
by torching the haystack
    not a poem, exactly
more like the one nameless container
superstitious sailors let circle the globe unopened
by which I mean it's ongoing
and includes among its contents
illicit parts that would need to be pulled out
and placed in proper relation
to other parts traveling alongside
a hopeless bargain with god

to create the weapon with which to maim
the very aspect of him that foresaw
and for some obscure reason permits it

>>

sun high but filtered
scents vegetal, bird and
bug song unhurried
twigs gray   and lichen
speckling their crooks light blue

big ant
scales my power cord
achieves the plug
prepares to mount the keyboard
I give it a decisive flick
we're both surprised when an instant later
it's flat against the windowpane
six feet away, intact and unharmed
or at least there's only a beat
before it goes its way across the glass
we'll meet again   don't bother fate

>>

smoked a Marlboro Gold
with distinct notes of walnuts and hard salami
    drew a picture and convinced her
to draw one too   delicacy is always the great revelation
    we got a speeding ticket
just when we'd been talking about how we'd do it
"I'd shoot myself in the head full of pills
while tumbling from the bridge"

no long, costly retreat   no being satisfied
with crumbs   though I love crumbs
and adore retreat   all those confessions made
on the blasted wagons someone already plans
to requisition in the chaos and recrimination that awaits
    cross broad and variegated country
having preemptively removed my uniform
per the survival manual
    unsung genre

>>

sure, I'd like to be dead
  touch the paintings in the museum
and be the supposedly intimate knowledge
of dynastic tugboat captains
in the shallows   and be the shallows

on the deck, mosquitos bite my thighs
and ankles   a strand of her hair attaches
itself to my face   with each cooling kiss
  I have to lean back a few extra inches
to get it to release and fall free

her favorite character in the comic is Cathexis
a.k.a. discharge itself, the genius of overflow
  we grow rotund with the substance
that knows our name, mutters it endlessly
and interrupts thoughts
obliged thereby to begin again
  what if my fantasies spill out
don't worry, they're attached to weights
and the weights attached to wrecks

>>

I switched places with the king   or was it really I
who switched places with the peasant?
  we'll meet in the climactic scene
to battle the multinationals side by side

if you knew how I've cried on that campus
  my daughter calls sobbing
because at dinner she was too shy
to even talk to her older cousins
  send them a message, I offer
a gust of revision ruffles the leaves

the nutritionist said imagine yourself as a book
  your gut flora the words   normalize
writing on the face   why are people
so determined to preen, prattle, or bicker
in public   and be so easily enjoined
by holidays, speeches, and shows?
  the clear thinkers I know
look increasingly pained

>>

learning makes me want
to sleep   you take the risk of being
buried with the expression that says
I understand, but I'm not going to help
    thanks for sticking around so at least
I could experience some anticipatory bliss

the book I'm reading is so full
I can squeeze it over my own page
    it says, be a stag, be hunted, the dogs
will free you from this nightmare of being whole
    you want a book of poems   but first
there must be a poem   "How could the invisible
return to being visible? By animating the drum.
The stretched skin of a dead animal was the steed,
it was the journey, the gilded whirlwind. It led
to the place where the grasses roar, where the rushes
moan, where not even a needle could pierce
the gray thickness"   Calasso, *The Celestial Hunter*

and from S's shelf   "The delicacy of that sense
of touch or audition by which the downy woodpecker
is enabled to locate those motionless insects in their hidden
burrow must ever command our admiration"

always the adequate symbol   fuck off
    though I suppose it's something
to discuss   nosing around a receptive neck
    passivity was frankly heaven
that night whose farthest reach we fathomed
    coming to in the taxi   my eyes
supposedly someone's ruin
at the taco truck   both the sky and I blushed

>>

were you supposed to be true to something?
and therefore to its lingering perfume?
it's easy to get confused   if you've been
to my cone, my pen, you know this
  it's easy to get confused by devices
and by whether it's true that when switched off
they can't observe or overhear us anymore
  even excitement baffles me   even a dynamo
said that   it's easy when in disgust
with fortune and men's eyes
to get confused in *Snow White*
when the small animals gladly kill themselves
so she can wear their fur   fox and sable
so soft they need to be fastened or
they'll slide right off her skin

my love wonders if
I'm present to change
  one treetop is highest in the sky
whorls of bark   the hummingbirds and
bored bees   great horned owl that would
snatch Slim if it could   my hearing
is worse, does that count   a soft spot for lambs
  hauntology in the boudoir
not just what's a moment, or who's this
but also is there a shred left of the shy kid
who would have been fascinated
if he'd known   and lurks in the corner, lately
a meek ghost   these days we despise
the shy   drag them into the street
to witness every degradation

>>

spent all night drawing continents
    next day added the faults   and endless
jade green waters, agitation increasing
as they cast their net of froth

we gasp when the porter steps aside
to reveal the splendor of the stateroom
aboard *The Celestial Queen*
but the logo on the notepad in the drawer
still reads *Unfinished Business*

while back in the city
in this modest civic triangle
whose paving stones the ambiguous energy of hand-holding
has forever permeated and charged   toddlers throw
shit fits   undercover cops shout FTP the loudest   literary agents
remain obsessed with world-building and poets, with light
    they can't help themselves   especially that mainstream one
who pitied me in a comment thread   best are the lines
that foresee a crisis   loiter at the scene
before it even arrives   then flash out like a pistol
to vouchsafe the people's report

>>

the time was defined
by protest
like the bike march that wove all through the city
chanting, what do we want?
justice
when do we want it?
now
at each corner trained volunteers blocked traffic
so our enormous organism could slide through
afterwards we drifted down toward
the base of the Brooklyn Bridge
where a bar served drinks to go
I offered to get a round, turned to my friends
so what do you guys want?
justice
that endless echo
since how can even the smallest decision be made
or make sense   in this maelstrom
we sat with the drinks, the fireworks
close and concussive overhead
it was morning when we finally biked
a final mile through Bushwick on spent legs
buses don't know how to pass cyclists
even on a deserted street

>>

pinned on avenues
still marked by barricades

robust shade
at Marsha P. Johnson State Park   some of us
are cute not cool   starved for touch the long
sick summer and all the beauty no one's seen
while it's been hidden away, available only
at some black market in caresses where for a price
you can be jostled by actors playing
straphangers, or wander into an ersatz store
to browse blank books

photographer wears a precision instrument
over her heart   the lone mercy
is to dig me out, up   when those ridiculous
involvements pointlessly end
and my face, in that picture   ingratiating
little shit   it wasn't me but my fingers
    they just wanted to text your fingers   invite them
to interlock at the cotillion

those distant piledrivers dismantle my ego, too
at a remove   every stratum of ruin proclaims
it rides the bedrock   I met that traitor down
at the public space the development corporation for
compliance's sake sulkily added   where the poor river
has to lick the matter-of-fact bank   in his version
I'm the deserter, taking my chances in a new nation
    never knowing certain childhood smells again
or rounding the same trusty corner
to the train

>>

someone left a hose running at the top of the path
    rivulet reflects a trickle of sky
one boxer holds up pads another pounds
    a kid rattles a stick against a fence
punctuated with a thud on the tree trunk at the end
    sweat prickles from exhausted pores   the remedy's
cool wind

fell off my bike and survived   got a new helmet
and a new seat   are we in danger, and refuse to see
this precise moment is where we fit
the component it requires
to resume its function   but where are you?
    in the past, fixated on your enlistment
in the future, yes, but how can you get there
without first materializing in the now?

it's true, my dearest belief was always
I'm not a part of that   whatever I gave
I retrieved at the last instant
by sleight of hand, so that in their hallways
companions wondered if they didn't in fact
have a hole in their pocket   patting their chests
and hips and asses for what I'd already repossessed
to hoard again   and kissed, too, the thread I admit
I've come to care about as much as the gem
it snatches surreptitiously back

>>

this isn't one of those free poems
everyone's always giving away
    I was sensible, and paid for it
took something that made my hands fret
    watched helpless as they worried the fringe of joy

I prep, try the reliable spots, wind up
overwhelmed by the festivity of others
    wish I could sit alone in a room and work, but work
is what unfolds here every moment
    frisbee players, three, how the disc rolls madly
when misthrown, uncaught   look at someone
until without exactly having glanced back
she fixes her shirt in a way unmistakably for me
    walks off with her friend
who carries a bag from Krispy Kreme
though we're five blocks from Peter Pan
and worse, with all this grubbing, nothing's sweet

>>

write epigrams   with an EpiPen
genuinely interested in these leaves of grass
quivering a bit   it makes you want to let the mind out
to try and extrapolate the total volume of flux
to understand all moments
if we call the sensation we summon
around fractal expansion *understanding*
since knowing without exactly feeling
seems a failure the spirit records

article reports no one can say how planes work
(a seaplane just kissed the river goodbye)
we engineer without being able to explain the fact of lift
while in the grass each auspice hides
perfectly among its clones
Con Ed station across the river
currently turns lavender and foregrounds
some slate-blue clouds too lazy to lift into the sky
if I were to design a building
it would look like my bike, laid on its side
and have no bathrooms, in honor of these afternoons

>>

try to keep a loose but exclusive village together
    and they me   sending messages
to which I respond partially   only occasionally
prompting someone to say   you are responding partially
    you are not entirely here   in truth
I am not entirely there   but we would like you
to be entirely here   I know, I know you would
and I am almost entirely there   but there is
a part of me   in spite of myself   that is there
in spite of myself
and another part wrapping heirlooms
and offerings in cloth bundles
to steal away and kneel with my head against
an ancient wall smeared with the yearning of pilgrims
to whisper energetically into its fissures
I can wait no longer, knock me down

>>

and fuck birthdays, too
    there's a kind of race on   one runner's jersey
displays a number that keeps changing
    while the other wears a t-shirt
that reads "will he ever say it?"

stoned with R   she discourses on the nature
of time   is it a substance, inside or
outside of us, is it shared?
    I confess we let my dad die, at least tacitly
so he wouldn't suffer for years to come
    "I was also gonna say . . ." "What?"
"I don't remember"
"You just said, 'I was also gonna say . . ."
"What were we talking about?"
"You said the time problem has two parts
then I said the thing about my dad
then you said 'I was also gonna say . . ."

>>

sorry I called you the queen of likes
who even cares, it's so silly
they're just, god, nothing, caprice, unless . . . ?
while we eat I choreograph mentally and in advance
packing up the trash on the table
we can't even recycle all our recycling
this paper has been what it absorbed
ink and food and shit
unless it came straight from the tree
and they tried to take the acid out of it
and I try to put it back in

>>

it’s feedback season   plant the seeds
we’ll harvest one day as form

ode to house readings
where someone always took notes   coterie poet
without the coterie   Sorrentino: “My youth is left
in the heads of a mere clique of people
who no longer know each other”
I’ve been trying to hang in there
with smarter, kinder people for most of my life
it was such a simple art then   telling them
how I adored their faces, their voices
used to write straight up the side of the page
in the heat of the chase, maybe still could

I miss you, I steal your style, it’s wonderful
I promise not to keep it too long

>>

we're in the city to study morphologies

think a lot about stone, metal, wood

can hardly keep up with what's alive and thriving

down that escarpment slippery with slime
a cattail maestro conducts the fronds
and a choir of these sort of half-open nuts
sing hosannas on trees that will weeks later dip and dance
with hanging bunches of light-violet fluted flowers
whose vessels look nearly orchid-like, head-on   help?

>>

are days with me so

my little rules and mania for repetition

looking at that old poem and thinking wow
it was just how I wanted it

the only parts of the city left are the gravel beds, the scree
condos wear long black veils   netting to interdict
what window washers drop
or window washers themselves

we all—why did I write *fear*—the river
now there's a rodeo in the clouds
fluffy gala, wrinkles in shirts
face down by the faucet   they're still at the table

if that drawing fell out of this notebook in McCarren, hoho

a lube called SPIT

>>

those talismanic volumes we carry
  X keeps *Crazy for Vincent* in her bag
Guibert's record of a nagging thrall to turn it into a book
he arranged the entries in reverse chronological order
so we could watch his resolutions unravel
and persecution turn to fuel like rewinding a forest fire
back into the column of a match

mini-genre of the two-sided film
Mulholland Drive, *Bergman Island, Tale of Cinema*, *Black Bear*
  all attuned to seduction of course you recall
the transformation of Naomi Watts in her audition
  and in *Black Bear* Aubrey Plaza reminds us what it means
for two people who have just met, have chemistry, and are
being watched to dare dance in a living room
  let alone touch hands

I can't even recommend things right you want lists
  I'm talking about terrain you must be traveling
by now through so many beds and berths
your summer journal will as a consequence
be compressed and neutral in that way
irresistible to strangers everywhere

>>

the tree outside the window
gives itself over to the wind
past the perfect shoulder
of my dissatisfied lover

fights   so smitten, I always
almost accidentally laugh   urge that must be
stifled at its source   before it can reach
the corners of the mouth

falsity, that black mold
    I bought these cutoffs *qua* cutoffs
one of the last days in a heavenly late summer
upon an increasingly agitated earth
beneath which our forebears stop throttling
one another only to gape confused at our amnesia
as if memory were itself an enormous
alphabetic sign, half-sunk in the mud
with no analogue in any living language
and nothing in the record
to which it might be compared

>>

shot our love scene with two cameras
then wanted to splice the parts together
but cherished each frame so much
that everything in the final edit occurs twice

we may yet live to see a hurricane
over a wildfire   spreading there
what it douses here   lifting
and hurling bolts of flame   failed
by the earth that goes mad
    failed by each other   and by myths
evergreen and strangely opaque
    this ambiguous passage
is said to recount either a harvest or a plague

summon the whirlwind
    if a pen goes dead mid-sentence
it's bad luck   if one explodes in your pocket
it means several years' prolific work
    superb, a whole day writing on a table
that's already been sold on craigslist
    across the way, the brownstone tips its blue cap

>>

the images I prize are exactly the ones
which can no longer pass through
the fine mesh filter each was issued by their brand

I don't care for what I've been served
so they send out even more   not quite the solution
  meanwhile my companion has chosen to acquiesce
to the eloquence of my grievance
but it keeps us from the business at hand, so we meet
the next day, and the next, delayed again by my complaints
  which is to say, the never-discharged
is inside me still, grinding like shrapnel against the bone
  and what leaks out from the damage
overpowers all other tastes

they call what you looked at your data
and of course, what you spent
  they let me teach
until I insisted everything
had been put in its place
  afterwards, there isn't any point

>>

could we share everything?

why do I think people are so bad?
they tell me they are

did you just litter?   I mean, a teabag
    finally we'll have the feelings
toss them from the fresh pit
while licking up whatever moonlight
manages to trickle down the muddy sides
past broken rocks and roots reaching for nothing
    to see the rim was all the invitation said

the cover's a rind   barcode a spot of decay
    bid online on a run of nights
we didn't use, back then
(one or both of us stayed in)
should I remove them
from their packaging?
see you in the bardo, formed like the tangle
your sticky hairs made with the dust
in the corner of the room   how I'd transport
the whole assemblage to the pail
and perform the dance of letting go

>>

now I’m in the same chair where this began
S is back on the road and left me, without
knowing it, a gift   an illustrated book about climbing
in Colorado, entitled *Climb!*, from 1977
the interviews are about the ethics
of the mountain   blah blah the unforgiving rock
the photos exquisite   almost exclusively men
probably aged 18-25   wedged into seams of granite
one partner always watches
from below, ready with the coiled rope
the only two full-color images are on the front and back covers
where okay yes the human glows against the stone

>>

episode in which a letter
sent by mistake or while intoxicated
or based on erroneous information
must be retrieved by bribe or break-in
before delivered

could it get too dark to write, out here?
but it's not the same as reading, I can write as big as I like
    feel the weights and am therefore easily outpaced

my god, your intelligence and complexity   a light gust
sends me a notification   whistling over the opening
of my empty ginger ale can   am I writing
in clay, or with smoke?   screenshot
the clouds   genius acquaintance posts a page
of Lessing   "The old watch the young
with anguish, pain, fear. Above all what each has learned
is what things cost, what has to be paid, the consequences
and results of actions. But their own lives have been
useless, because nothing they have learned
can be passed on"

it got too dark to write

>>

birdfeeder party   everyone's tiny heart
beats madly with excitement   can't say I recognize
those gray corsairs in black helmets
with a few modest stripes on their shoulders
whose takeoffs and landings
sway the tube, scattering what some chipmunks
gather below   and bluebird, bully, I wait a long time
but won't be fast enough to photograph
those wings open to full lattice pattern
    display it never sees   yet knows
its entire being to be

knotted cords hang like quipus around the conservatory
from a cross-cord strung across the top   I theorize
they prevent birds from thinking the glass panes
a shimmer of air

an acorn hit the deck so loud
that at first I checked the china and crystal in the cabinets
for a spontaneous break
    later ascertain it was not an acorn
but some impregnable nut

the eclecticism of a house
that is itself a large thought   as the best ones are
    includes a design-piece lamp beside
a dish that must be family silver
    maybe belonging to the man with muttonchops
whose portrait graces the office where the bulk of the library
is adventure tales for every latitude
    a whole shelf's dedicated to Antarctica alone
genre of cold, of suffering   of giving up
only to desperately persist   of mutinies
and the call of the sea
    disappearance, gender, madness
near the hidden antennae of the Earth

>>

thirsty   in a glass room
in steady rain
    have some peach juice   sip of nectar

the trees look as though projected on scratched film
and even when the sun returns
it's ten degrees colder in the house than in the yard
    try the boggy back deck
then the front lawn, equipped
with pens phone cigarettes matches tea
    google, wait, do wind chimes play *do re mi*?
the staples hug the folded pages oh so close
    the notebook a wide-open mouth
with my pen I'm the dentist   scraping around inside

I have these implements for company
and through them, you, hearing this poem and texting
me after that you liked it   if you think me
above such pleasures, no   if anything
that's me at my most refined

>>

hadn't meant to watch *Certain Women* again
    but this time it haunted me all night

sad, majestic Montana   entanglements
play out against the mountain range   stark
and omnipresent on the horizon
    in the first two episodes women engage
in give-and-take with men   Laura Dern's lawyer
is fed up with her client until she realizes
he has in fact been screwed by the system, as he claims
    she surprises him and herself and us, moving
from irritated duty to exasperated care

in the next part Michelle Williams
feels guilty cajoling the pile of sandstone
from René Auberjonois   though by the end
she'll appraise the material stacked neatly on
the site of the house she's building   fish out
a cigarette, drink wine from a plastic cup
    realize she made the right choice
to redeem what he wouldn't or couldn't

>>

still, it's the episode between the two women
that runs the deepest   Lily Gladstone works her winter job
caring for horses at a ranch   she's impossibly solitary
    almost complete unto her silence
until one night, by a chance that's more than chance
she wanders into the school
because she sees others going in
    turns out they attend a class in school law
and she is tempted into their community
only because that dangerous space is filled
by the immanence of the instructor, Kristen Stewart
whom she joins for a bite to eat, afterwards
though Gladstone doesn't eat a thing   such activities
mean nothing to her   she is at the edge of this world
for Stewart, who doesn't engage, just grumbles
about her hours-long commute to this secondary gig
but also somehow permits the moment to exist   which seems sufficient
    it goes on this way for a few weeks   finally Gladstone arrives
to class astride one of the horses, sitting proud and tall
    Stewart climbs on the saddle behind her   they ride to the diner
then at the very next session there's a sub, it's understood Stewart
won't be back   without a thought Gladstone drives all night
and by early morning waylays Stewart in the parking lot of her job
    an entirely unbearable encounter ensues
Stewart knows but doesn't address what's happening
    Gladstone in the midst of her grand gesture
but faced with unspoken rejection made worse by pity
remains polite and deferential   even as she is annihilated
    now the wild life of the animals to which she returns
is reconfigured as a senseless void
    to have desired and grasped is to have let in
a different kind of meaning and with it
the risk of its utter dispersal
    like planting dead seed

>>

Slim wakes me at six am
    hue and girth of these pills   the flume ride
they take down the throat
    big branch on the garage roof
and leaves and acorns on the deck chairs
    wind chimes cathedral bells
last night tried to hear the owls
say “who cooks for you?”   sang Slim’s name
as he trailed me through the rooms

it’s work, manufacturing temptations to crime
    knew better than to slide down
the slope of these compromises
to wear out these pleasures
but did it anyway
the consequences, long-deferred, now arrive
    we’re bound to the tracks   the moon
watches a blood-red sun descend
    bug I swat leaves a phosphorescent streak

to kill a fly   open your hands a foot above it
and begin to bring them together
    by the time it arrives
you’ll intercept it   this requires faith   overcoming
what feels like it will end in empty-handedness
    no one wants to be empty-handed   besides, the fly
is perceptive, dazzlingly fast
except you know where it’s going before it does
and you yourself are perceptive   dazzlingly fast
    remember your fate knows not only where you are
but where you will be   nor does it appreciate
clapping its powerful hands on emptiness
    you’ll have to decide not to retreat after all
but linger, without resources, in the shadow
of the city walls, eating what the little prince
you once were would never have deigned to eat

>>

to make a discovery's not easy   first you have to
push a question out of your mouth   kid in the past
who wove together from available threads
a memory out of some unassuming moment
to which he wouldn't think to return as an adult
except perhaps by means of a physical awakening
that might allow him to perceive at last
how it was never the purpose of the memory to suggest
by its apparently unaccountable persistence
a return to itself, for itself   but rather that,
in returning to it, one finds and gather the threads
from which the memory was originally woven
because they would dangle there still   like cables
of silk   rich and unfaded   nature being fine
or who am I kidding   it always brings its best

>>

I fumble, in this beautiful but unfamiliar house
   get the bathroom floor wet   burn damp logs
instead of taking from the dry pile
as the note warned I should
   slip down the stairs, idiot
but at the bottom nothing's broken
   night's soft, in total darkness
sleep like a dead man, and resist in my dreams
the howling of the cat   even concocting a dream cat
just so that I might feed and quiet it
   yesterday the skunk with a white mullet ignored me
while it feasted on nuts that fell and bounced
into the zone of its gleaning

I drive these improbably unspoiled environs
   stop to photograph a tree whose
yellow leaves, ovals with sharp ends, are as if half-dipped in red
   see egrets, think of Anselm
open my car door   clatter of yerba mate cans tumbling out

from *Climb!*   "He placed a knife blade piton
in a thin crack, but felt that the protection it gave
was purely psychological"   on camping trips I'm the last to leave
a fire until it's nothing but pulsing orange powder   all things soil-
bound are alive, penetrative, grinding   there's a nucleus
inside each particle and a partisan unslinging a rifle
behind every thicket   "the rumble of panic
underneath everything" (Ernest Becker)

if you see the invisible
it's because a message is poised to arrive   Calasso says
shamans live in a larch with many levels, branch to branch
they do not die a natural death
but are only ever swallowed up
in the struggle with another shaman

he contends the Milky Way is a midden   a celestial liver
or waste heap above which vultures circle   an airport at the outskirts
anyone here must be passing through

>>

you ask what evenings in this place are like
    music, but not the witless kind   weather, naked   drinks
without the sprites   who long since escaped the bottles

if only we could grab a happy-hour nectar at Topaz
    the way I tell our story now
like I'm daring someone to object

glory begins in gossip, let them talk   and don't try
the trick where you say your name is Nobody
    he already knows, devours nobodies by the gross

some names are so specific
if they appeared on the face of my ringing phone
a current would turn my spine from bone to a sword
still glowing in the forge   and the voice
on the other end would be the ice-cold bath
into which it's plunged

>>

exciting object   doorknob doubled
by tears   stack of papers
thrown in the air
comes down and covers the river
    flat on the surface it makes a floe
passing under the bridge   and the final
shot wanders unaccountably at first
to trace the structure's central pylon
up towards the top corner of the screen
    as we close in, a form emerges in relief
from the graven adornments   an interruption
so slow   that even the universe
would admit   it hovers

>>

careworn and anxious   reach out
to pinch the lamp’s black plastic stem
and twist it by its ridged head to off

you get the drift, at some point the books
on the shelves are longer than your life
    too long to revisit   the paintings’
emanations too arresting to look away

it’s inconceivable that we die and they put us in the earth
    it’s just unbelievable that I can’t have what I want
only gape forever at its inexhaustible mineral hue
    its departure on the solar wind   but then sometimes
though there’s still the pinprick of its not-quite vanishing
    forget to follow where it goes

>>

people get themselves made into characters
in books they probably wouldn't like
    Guibert's lover Vincent, for example
who thought he was hustling jobs and girls
    taking drugs toward ever-better highs   jerking
a rich boyfriend off and around   when in fact
he was being written or really, moved in the way
writing likes to approach   one of those fascinating
brutes, sometime poets whose poetry is to hold
a hushed conversation at the level of the skin
that's always dying into sheets and onto the floor
but also registers signs of presence   the mark of nails
or teeth   not to speak of its colloquy with the blood

>>

the smells of London
or of Paris streets

the different air   lost analog paradise
    sailors in a time when information
couldn't move faster than a ship   thoughts faster
than the application of ink

the library in *Wings of Desire*
    books spend eternities closed   taxonomy of
what people think I know, or don't

secret delicious pleasures, like telling someone
in the middle of an argument
actually they're totally right about everything

>>

jealousy, ten-armed, hundred-eyed
and each eye a screen

dream in which
one's love has a lover, and together
they eat bread   they go to bed
and in the dazzling
mental shorthand of that state
dispatch a message

walk the rooms, closing
the closet doors she always leaves open
    finding too much finality perhaps
in that last emphatic push

>>

the first rule is that above all
it can't be done
as it was the time before
and so one diverts, and though the repertoire
of possible acts seems limited   somehow
variations appear, lead elsewhere   always
to a different sensation   and then beyond this
are the ever-changing scents, the softening
or hardening of bodies   unpredictable evolution
of curiosities and tastes   until there's no way of revisiting
the original pleasures, exactly
    we started somewhere and now are far distant
like travelers who met on a journey and don't yet know
where or when they'll part (but know they must)
    meanwhile my hand, wedged under my ribs
starts to ache, I fling it awkwardly off the bed

in the casino where chips represent years
a player pushes stacks across the green felt

when I was her refuge   when one of us woke
every few hours   to paw the other
then sink back into half-sleep to recover

>>

what do people really think of each other
  I know, because they tell me

why complain to the entire town?
  to defuse all possible gossip

oh you are not like him, says one
  ugh   that face   which is what we have to go on
say you're doing well   makes it difficult to   outline a novel or
vivify the arcane   I lose the poem   in the poem's
headlong rush   it passes me, then claims
to be mine   and the claim I had   if I say
I see it   in your mind   and hear it between the lines
  nothing's more inarticulate than poets at the end
of the night   rubbing each other's heads   taking photos
  shaking emptiness out of their wallets
the words we want to catch   only emerge when they're together
  when what was locked in each person in their multiplicity
begins to purr   everyone's demands sent reeling   not a fantasy
but brief as one   leaving an unbearable, eloquent silence
  its artifacts mysterious, enigmatic   and the urge to deny it
strong to the point of zeal   when morning arrives
  like knocking over a whole set of drums

>>

I'd hate to have to write the book
explaining an absence
the absence of writing
could never hold

we seek validation but it's impossible
    even the person who leaves us for nothing but misery
doesn't appear on the doorstep one day
saying you were right, I wish I hadn't gone

go ahead and print caution on both sides of the tape
catch a teardrop falling toward a letter
with a dagger
    did she glimpse, at some point, the flash of the trait
that would one day disappoint her, in him   the first moment
when he was supposed to be looking at her
but was looking elsewhere instead
    I see your beauty, he can't   who cares
about beauty, anyway? I shout to the gallery
    they all look down, ashamed

is anyone else experiencing certain references as violent blows?
    those bad artists cinch it   no amount of labor
or desire can make you quick   whereas psychosis is a wand
beneath which syntax breaks into warnings and baffling hints

the two kinds of products
delirium-objects   and shame-objects
    often sold as a matched set

>>

my daughter says her favorite part
is when Neo yeets into the agent

finally on the other side of discernment
  barren and dark as those moons without atmosphere
whose soil touches outer space   sifts, nearly
detaches, comes to rest

slogans, riddles, info dump   a drink
to involve me in the energy of the street
  charming dents and dimples visible
today   biking in 57-degree weather
is like traveling through time
in my two-bit fashion, at least

cold nights in Binghamton, in Providence
  mid-November, an excellent season to think
outdoors, romping across the quad   it felt crazy, falling
into that bush   it was everywhere
and I was hurting it, too   heard the cracks
of a thousand twigs, or sub-twigs

last blue of afternoon   a delicate fill
  I've been on the whole journey
already   down and back up (funny old gummy)
  what heaven it would be
to eat a light dinner then head out   grab a quiet
drink alone   show up to the party
a bit spent but easily recharged   catch up
with some friends   maybe see who's planning
to linger late   and wind up swinging my gate
in instead of out at dawn

>>

met a pretty piano teacher, tried and failed
to flirt   maybe she loves her partner and kids?
    their meaningful life?
did miss the holidays in the city
    crush of signification and desire
out of which coincidences precipitate
like the holy snow

think a lot lately about Nedra
and the underground river   her image
for the journey of middle age, made alone and unseen
    I've read *Light Years* so many times
the chapters are rooms into which one is welcomed
with a discreet wave, and enters hat in hand
    sometimes I read only the parts where he loves
Kaya Doutreau   the bathtub, the museum, the break-up
    then years later he spots her across
a restaurant, unexpectedly   and after his heart stops
and time collapses, his first impulse is to hide somehow
because imagine being seen on the far side
of those total and disastrous wagers
what Catherine and Heathcliff learn in that garden
    you only get one chance to meet again

>>

have you ever seen   but why
would you have   you don't
know tedium   the life of
a nail, once driven

a patient, I moan
that nothing flows out of me
    wary of speech after
so much silence
    I like your highlights
I noticed, I'd just forgotten to exist

was saying have you seen
not transformation
but its scouts ride through?
    if you even flinch they hear
and then it comes in force
to spoil your crops and wells

to say something and then say it
again a bit differently   long dream
of writing, infinitely long
    in the sanctuary where poems
are pulled free as half-healed
scabs from skin   followed by
a flash of red   the gods, though
bloodless, reserve the right to blush
    before unleashing some
appalling display of setting right
what was momentarily
and in their name overthrown

>>

unfold the shutters
but the room stays cold

I feel it, sober as I am
not belonging in the world anymore
though I'd like to watch
a movie of one of those gatherings
where belonging happened   if only
such a movie existed

car in mud   car on ice
    how satisfying to push and feel the wheels
grip the street, the chassis float away
from beneath one's gloves

chafe my hands   the pan
retains a rind of food   the counter a ring
from the mug   the part of the arm
that dangles   folds of the neck
    the optic nerve   strains against
its master   toward the deadpan room

they closed the bars
so I deface my own bathroom walls
    "you can't fool me"   now we're really on
Cold Mountain, I say to nobody, after years
on Cold Mountain, where rain makes
the tin roof sing   varnishes branches black
and plumps their tips   all seasons in a single night
    underwater or under-wine

marsh gives way to prairie   a field guide
to moths   a field guide to gallery goers
whose perfect self-assurance in the realm of value
turns to ether the railing

upon which an oil rig worker leans
so that the next moment he tumbles
into the steaming sea

>>

what occurred gnaws at what's permitted

what's permitted makes a brutal example of what's occurred

how each thing will end   each task, day, phase, and con
    the dishes piled with food   are also dishes
to be done   tell me to stop hurrying through it
place your hand
on the back of my neck
    source from which relief must emanate
with an initial jolt (how I miss the train)

fourth-down play drawn in the palm
    there was a moment when my mind
wanted discipline   in the minutes before sleep
I taught it to dig a well now deep enough
to touch water that's never seen the light of day
nor floated free of the earth
    it tastes like smoke and coins

>>

the set teeters   behind the stage
nature waits   not the gentle kind

there's a saddle of gravel
on the side of this frozen mountain
at a switchback of the road
where we smoke in the blinking light of the hazards
look out over the tops of trees
watch the wind fluff the firs
    as over some unknown orifice
it mimics the howl of a wolf
    take a last glance around
as only our defeated species can
    get back in the car   toward somewhere
in the boundless country where no one
knows us   and we're bound together
for once in the same plane of existence
and for once traversing it at the same pace

what we call the comet is the comet's undoing
    no speck of it won't, before the climax
express a vector gravity imposed
just as our talk spends us, and cannot exactly
pull free from the sheer density
of so much participation

it's for the best our true souls
are disguised in the human, in the social
    it wouldn't do any good, after all
to behold someone's true form
twenty feet tall   on second ave   flaying
the adversary who begs for it, taunts
the effort, and all the while admires,
despite himself, the trophies dangling
on a line around that pitiless throat

>>

there’s that apocryphal variant of Icarus
    he catches his father quickly hiding
some tools one day   Dedalus rushes off
but now I, out on the pier, realizes he’s going to try
something crazy, what no one’s ever done, for precisely
this reason   he leaps and reaches up   and wouldn’t
you know it, comes down having pinched the sun
out of the sky   it was only a small disk
tacked right above, pretending by puppetry to cross
the heavens   sticks it in his satchel, the world goes
instantly dark   he trips off the edge   cracks his head
and topples into the waves   then something something
    the rushes the reeds   like Ophelia
drifting and snagging all the way down the shallow stream

>>

can’t stop laughing when Michelle Williams
with uncontrollable trembling tells him
“My heart was broken . . . it’s always gonna be broken”

we must imitate to change, says this chapter
    and once we change, lose what came before
unless we have been very careful with our initiation

afraid to look back through these pages
folded up like those medieval shutters in the day
    at night you can tell which panels were replaced

how terrible in therapy, what happens to my voice
when I feel invited to tell the truth

obviously there’s a voice you’d use in the desert
if you were there long enough
    forget the first ten years spent apologizing to the rocks

had it at the start, lost it in the confusion
    all that’s left to see is how it looks
when things catch up to people
and reveal them   the trappings gone
the way an escaped animal finally sheds
whatever bits of plastic or leather vouchsafed its period
under guard, glove, or yoke

a superstition about never filling a notebook to the end
and a compulsion to raise into pyramids the pods
of half-and-half when waiting in a booth

tell the hummingbirds
bring sugar to my demise
    when I close my eyes

the chandelier hangs
in green and purple negative
inside the lids

>>

the thing I'm looking for
is so small, and disappears so quickly
   indestructible and proud

if you believe in magic, don't resist cycles
   don't forget Eros also shoots lead-tipped arrows
that drive love away from their victim
and Guibert dreams there's an evil spell
that once cast makes the person you love
withdraw at your approach

Calasso says the mysteries
are neither a thought to be possessed
nor a formula to be applied
   they are, rather, to be experienced
at Eleusis   and how can one return there?
by leaving, by going back to ordinary life
then waiting for the call

after these disappointments, we'll attempt
a seedy art again   without nourishment
   against taste

lurk in the old districts, waiting for justice
to ring out   and at that signal
the air explodes with unbridled color

only then will we grasp those possibilities
   to turn away, to stay

>>

8:30, pitch-dark, the workers finally finish up
    I watch from my window
as one pulls the truck away from the curb   his partner
cleans the spot where it spent the day   scrapes at hardened
white starbursts of plaster with a flat shovel
    brushes the particles into piles with a stiff broom
(the sounds carry up to me) and deposits them
in a plastic bucket he hoists
into the bed to cart off

parking is so hard around here
yet sometimes in total excitement or perversion
we drive right past an empty spot

NOTES

Chantal Akerman (p. 51) is cited in Lucas Ferraço Nassif's *Missing Links: A book in ten sessions* (Barakunan, 2024). The passage from Anne Carson (p. 53) appears in *Autobiography of Red* (Vintage, 1998). Gilbert Sorrentino's "Poem" (p. 91) appears in his *New and Selected Poems 1958-1998* (Green Integer, 2004). The quote from Doris Lessing (p. 100) is from her novel *Shikasta* (Knopf, 1980).

ACKNOWLEDGMENTS

Versions of some of these poems appeared in *Poetry*, *The Brooklyn Rail*, *e-flux journal*, *18 Owls*, *NOMATERIALISM*, *Long News*, *Antiphony*, and *A Perfect Vacuum*.

I'm grateful to the entire visionary team at Nightboat Books, and especially for the continued support and boundless talents of Kit Schluter. For generosity and wise counsel, thank you Alexis Almeida, Lily Gurton-Wachter, Litia Perta, and Susan Fox Rogers.

This book is for Malka Longabucco and Rachel Valinsky—iridescent loves.

MATT LONGABUCCO is the author of the poetry collections *The Hummingbird* and *Heroic Dose*, as well as *M/W: An essay on Jean Eustache's* La maman et la putain, a book-length study of a landmark of French cinema and its creator.

NIGHTBOAT BOOKS

Nightboat Books, a nonprofit organization, seeks to develop audiences for writers whose work resists convention and transcends boundaries. We publish books rich with poignancy, intelligence, and risk. Please visit nightboat.org to learn about our titles and how you can support our future publications.

The following individuals have supported the publication of this book. We thank them for their generosity and commitment to the mission of Nightboat Books:

Kazim Ali, Anonymous (4), Ava Aviva Avnisan, Wilson Baldridge, Jean C. Ballantyne, Rumeli Banik, Will Blythe, Nick Buffon, Rob Byrnes, Martha Chowning & Jonathan Groff, V. Shannon Clyne, Juliana Cobb, Theodore Cornwell, Gisela Gamper, Photios Giovanis, Janlori Goldman, Amanda Greenberger, David Groff & Clay Williams, Daniel Handler, Sarah Heller, Karen Holtzman, Parag Rajendra Khandhar, Shari Leinwand, Elizabeth Madans, Bruno Franco Medeiros, Pooja Mehta, Ethan Mitchell, Caren Motika, Elizabeth Motika, Zehra N, Asker Saeed, Mark Sexton & Kirk Wallace, The Leslie Scalapino - O Books Fund, Amy Scholder, Chloe Silverman, Eric Suchyta, James Voorhies, Jerrie Whitfield & Richard Motika

This book is supported, in part, by a grant from the Poetry Foundation, in addition to public funds from the New York City Department of Cultural Affairs in partnership with the City Council, and the New York State Council on the Arts with the support of the Office of the Governor and the New York State Legislature.

POETRY FOUNDATION NYC Cultural Affairs NEW YORK STATE OF OPPORTUNITY. Council on the Arts